TRANSPORT OF
ITALIAN ART EXHIBITS
ANGLO-ITALIAN EXPRESS
EVAN COOK'S
B-8528

THE ILLUSTRATED HISTORY OF

Leyland

TRUCKS

NICK
BALDWIN

Foulis

Haynes

A **FOULIS** Motoring Book

First published 1986

Published by:
Haynes Publishing Group
Sparkford, Nr. Yeovil, Somerset
BA22 7JJ, England

Haynes Publications Inc.
861 Lawrence Drive, Newbury Park,
California 91320 USA

**British Library Cataloguing in
Publication Data**

Baldwin, Nick
    The illustrated history of Leyland
    trucks.
    1. Leyland trucks – History
    I. Title
    '629.2'24   TL230.5.F48

    ISBN 0-85429-575-5

Library of Congress catalog card
number 86-82628

Editor: Robert Iles
Page layout: Tim Rose
Printed in England by: J.H. Haynes & Co.
Ltd.

Introduction

The story of Leyland is very much the story of the British truck industry. Leyland was in at the beginning and grew and prospered as steam and petrol vehicles gradually ousted the horse from heavy haulage.

Few motor firms in the world have had such a classic beginning. Many were spawned by the Victorian technology and precision engineering that made it possible to mass-produce sewing machines, bicycles and then motorised transport. Leyland's predecessor, the Lancashire Steam Motor Company, on the other hand, owed its origins to the village blacksmith in Leyland, located in Lancashire away from the new light industrial centres of Coventry and London. Its first experiments with steam powered vehicles began as early as 1880, and production lorries were turned out from 1896.

A prototype lorry powered by an internal combustion engine in 1904 led to a change of direction and the steamers were slowly neglected, though not finally abandoned until the mid 1920s.

In 1907 the company was reformed following the takeover of Preston-based steam rivals Coulthards, and subsequently retitled Leyland Motors Ltd. Instead of continuing to buy its petrol engines from Crossley, the new firm took the plunge and introduced its own. These were fine power units for their time and contributed to Leyland's success with fire engines from 1910. Soon afterwards, Leyland became one of the earliest firms to be selected to build vehicles for the War Office subvention scheme. Some 6000 of the famous RAF type Leylands performed splendidly in the First World War. Many were rebuilt after the war at the newly acquired Kingston-on-Thames factory outside London and went on to perform equally inportant roles in civilian haulage, where many were still employed 20, or even 30, years later.

The Kingston factory gave Leyland a chance to explore the lighter vehicle field, first with the Trojan and then in the 1930s with the Cub and Lynx ranges.

Meanwhile, in Lancashire the factories returned to full production in the mid 1920s after many postwar difficulties. Following the introduction of some of the best buses and coaches of the day, came a brand new series of truck models with animal names, launched in late 1928. These were immensely successful, especially after the first of Leyland's diesel engines was announced in 1931, and from 1933 virtually all Leylands could be diesel powered. This marked the beginning of an expansionist phase, with fleets of Leyland being sold all over the world. The company's products also took the lion's share of the British heavy truck market, with AEC providing the only major competition in this field.

After building trucks and tanks in the Second World War, Leyland introduced its Comet 'world truck' and the company's climb into the international league began, first with the purchase of Albion in 1951, then Scammell in 1955. The merger with its long-standing rivals AEC in the early 1960s and the subsequent link with BMC are outlined in the later picture captions.

The history of Leyland is a vast subject and the firm has built an extraordinary diversity of vehicles in the past hundred years. In selecting photographs to illustrate this complex story, I have gone for variety and interest. With the vehicles of so many acquired truck firms to choose from, I decided to limit descriptions to vehicles that actually came to be known as Leylands. To cover all the trucks of AEC, Thornycroft, Maudslay, Guy, Austin, Morris, Albion, Scammell, etc. would have required a book ten times this size. I intend to return to these individual makes in future titles in this series of books.

In the meantime, I hope you will enjoy the nostalgic views of transport long ago and be as fascinated as I was by some of the unusual vehicles that have been produced in recent years. There are, of course, plenty of pictures of the familiar vehicles that have helped to make the Leyland name so famous on trucks throughout the twentieth century.

Acknowledgements

My thanks to everyone who helped with the preparation of this book. Many of the pictures were accumulated over a long period by my late colleague Prince Marshall. He, more than anyone, popularised the older commercial vehicle through his magazine "Old Motor" and was a very enthusiastic preservationist. Leyland was one of the subjects planned for our joint MHB books and it is very pleasing that Haynes/Foulis should have taken over the series and made this the first of the new titles.

I am also grateful to Nick Georgano who, like me, has equal enthusiasm for cars and commercials, and who tracked down the middle eastern model shown later in the book. We are both Trustees of the Michael Sedgwick Memorial Trust, which is an extremely worthwhile body set up to further research into motoring history and to help publish works that might otherwise not be commercially viable. Contributions will be gratefully received by Brian Heath, 20 High Street, Milford on Sea, Lymington, Hants. Michael Sedgwick was arguably the finest motoring historian of all and interestingly enough he was another who had a high regard for commercial vehicles and who would have liked to see Leyland trucks receive the historical attention that they deserve.

1. The village blacksmith in Leyland, Lancashire, was run by the Sumner family. In the early 1880s they built a steam vehicle for carrying five ton loads of coal to nearby Stanning's bleachworks. It was not a success and a political rival used this poster in his successful campaign against Stanning and his 'road destructor'.

2. Having built a few light steam pleasure vehicles and lawn mowers, J. Sumner Ltd changed its name in 1896 to the Lancashire Steam Motor Company, by which time it was employing 20 men. Finance was provided by the Spurrier family, who also had an interest in the Coulthard steam vehicle firm.

This famous photograph shows Henry Spurrier Junior at the tiller of the first 'Leyland' wagon in 1896. It had a two-cylinder compound 10/14 hp engine and could carry 1$\frac{1}{2}$ tons.

3. The first wagon sold commercially was this three tonner of 1897. The purchaser was Fox Bros of Wellington, Somerset, who used it to collect wool from depots in a nine mile radius. Like other early products of the Lancashire Steam Motor Co. it had a paraffin-fired boiler.

4. By 1899 the wagons had grown to four tonners and the one shown here won the premier award at the Liverpool Trials that year. Note the brake shoes that worked directly on the steel rear tyres.

5. In 1901 Leyland sent three of these post vans to Ceylon — their first exports. Paraffin fuel was giving way to coal and coke at this time. 40 wagons had been made by 1903 and the following year's output was 33. The workforce had grown to 160 and the factory site to three acres.

6. The first petrol-engined prototype appeared in 1904 and was this 1^1/$_2$ tonner nicknamed the Pig. It had a two-cylinder 12 bhp engine with worm drive. Production versions for three to five tons followed in 1905.

7. About 30 steamers a year were made in the 1905-7 period. In 1907 the rival Coulthard firm was acquired and the combined business retitled Leyland Motors Ltd.

8. An Edwardian 25 cwt post van with 24 hp engine by Crossley, who were suppliers for many of Leyland's early petrol chassis. 16 petrol vehicles were sold in 1905, 27 in 1906 and 17 in 1907.

9. A local operator in Preston, H. Viney and Co. Ltd, had built up this impressive fleet by about 1910. All are Leylands except the Taskers 'Little Giant' traction engine on the left.

10. George V became king in 1910 and was supplied with a 30 hp shooting van that year by Leyland. A Royal Warrant was granted and this baggage van was delivered in the following year.

11. Leyland made their own L-head engines from 1910 and they must have been good as this 1912 three tonner shown here was still in service in 1930. One would have thought that the low-slung radiator would have been vulnerable to damage.

12. Carter Paterson's fleet of X types lasted right up to 1932 when the one on the extreme left was preserved by Leyland. Some are shown here in a 1926 CMUA parade alongside a 'modern' Vulcan. Another Leyland that has survived from this era is Leicester Industrial Museum's 1911 tower wagon, used by Leicester Corporation tramways until 1949 and thereafter in their depot.

13. The X series was introduced in 1907 and, when this chassis was photographed in 1909, was available in capacities of 3¹/₂ to five tons using a six litre four-cylinder engine. There were four forward gears with direct top.

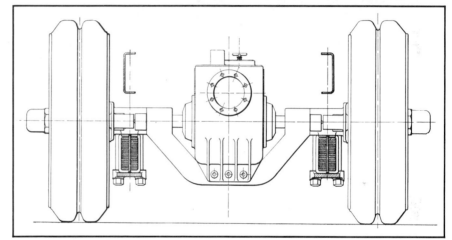

14. Drive axles had bevel gearing in a separate cast steel casing bolted to the forged load-carrying portion. Shown is a 5/6 ton type, whilst the three tonner had overslung springs. There was a torque tube and patent spherical thrust bracket.

15. Overtype versions of most of the early petrol range were made. This is one in later life looking battered and rather strange with hurricane lamps for illumination. In 1913, Leyland bought a 25 acre site at Farington for expansion and was making steamers and fire engines at Chorley. The workforce had grown to about 1500.

16. The Borough of Chelsea bought at least two dozen steamers between 1900 and 1906 and the adjoining Royal Borough of Kensington also had a substantial fleet. In this photograph a refuse collector is being hand-tipped. The ladder was carried on the wagon to make loading from bins possible.

17. Fire appliances were built from 1909 and construction of 85 hp six-cylinder machines began in the following year. This was a 55 hp escape supplied to Tasmania in 1913.

18. A Leyland 'Patent Vacuum Extractor' or gully emptier. It had a capacity of five tons and was supplied in 1914. By the outbreak of war in the same year, Leyland had sold a total of almost 2100 vehicles since 1896.

19. In 1912 Leyland became one of the first manufacturers of three ton vehicles to gain approval under the War Office Subsidy scheme. Operators were paid to keep the machines in fit condition for call-up. Here is one shortly before the Great War.

20. The War Office had bought a few petrol Leylands from 1907 and placed 'colossal' orders totalling 88 vehicles in 1912/13. When war came orders were stepped up and Subsidy vehicles requisitioned. Here we see an assortment of types including a former charabanc on the left.

21. The Subsidy Leylands achieved fame in the First World War with the Royal Flying Corps (later RAF). They became universally known as RAF types and about 5400 were supplied to the air force, including 765 of these travelling workshops.

MOTORS L^{TD}

2 MT Convoy
...t Pass 1918

22. 127 special two tonners were built for the Indian Army in 1914/16. Several of them were used for carrying supplies up the Khyber Pass and survived several years of alternate boiling and freezing conditions on the 18 mile climb.

17

23. (Five pictures). In all, 5932 Leylands were built for war service (including 144 released for essential civilian purposes) and many more were requisitioned. They had 32, 36 or 40 hp four-cylinder petrol engines and water-cooled transmission brakes. Here we see a sectioned chassis and a small assortment of vehicles in service in Britain and abroad, where they earned an enviable reputation for reliability.

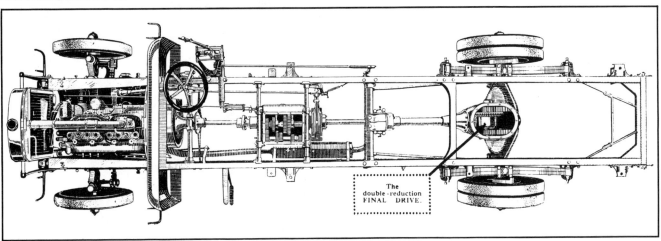

The
double-reduction
FINAL DRIVE.

24. The Leyland Motor Company had been reconstructed in 1914 with a capital of £400,000, flourished through the Great War, and was employing 3800 men in the immediate postwar years. However, demand for new vehicles slumped and by the end of 1922 losses of £1 million had accrued. Ex-War Office types were damaging sales and Leyland decided to buy as many as possible for reconditioning, both to make money and to avoid sub-standard vehicles damaging their reputation. Here we see some of the approximately 3000 that passed through the old Sopwith aircraft factory that they had acquired at Ham, Kingston-on-Thames.

Pulling the **Leyland** R·A·F to pieces – and putting it together again

Reconditioning as a fine art –

25. After a lapse of six years, construction of steam wagons recommenced at Chorley in 1920 and continued until 1926, when the spares were sold to Atkinson. A total of about 900 had been made by the time production ceased. Here we have another of Viney's fleet hauling a tram in about 1920.

26. The postwar 3-6 tonners sold slowly until supplies of RAF types were used up. Most were similar to their predecessors but a few were produced for both goods and passenger service as rather top-heavy looking cabovers, or overtypes as Leyland preferred to call them. In 1923 the forward-control driving position was brought down alongside the engine on the six tonner instead of over it and Leyland described this as a side type!

27. A handsome pair of fire appliances in London in 1919. Demand for these and for new goods vehicles was generally small in the early 1920s, which led Leyland to concentrate on selling buses. In 1925 their famous Lion and other L series psvs appeared. For five years from 1923 Leyland made the Trojan car and van at Kingston, though less successful was the Leyland luxury car designed by chief engineer J.G. Parry Thomas, of which less than 20 were sold.

28. In 1923 there appeared a much smaller vehicle than had previously been produced by Leyland except the vans of its Trojan subsidiary. This Z type had pneumatic tyres, a 20 hp overhead camshaft engine, and was for $1\frac{1}{2}$ ton loads. Very few were built and for the rest of the 1920s Leyland concentrated on vehicles for two tons and upwards.

29. An attractive 1925 Leyland 2/3 tonner with 32 hp engine. By the end of that year the cumulative losses had been reduced to £710,000 and were cleared after two years. Dennis was far more prosperous than Leyland in this period and considered a takeover in 1929; a Leyland/AEC merger was contemplated soon afterwards.

30. The RAF type was the backbone of hundreds of transport fleets. Quite apart from the 2939 reconditioned by Leyland and 171 that needed no work on them, many more were purchased direct by garages and transport men, in addition to most of the spares originally supplied to the government. (more on pages 24 to 27)

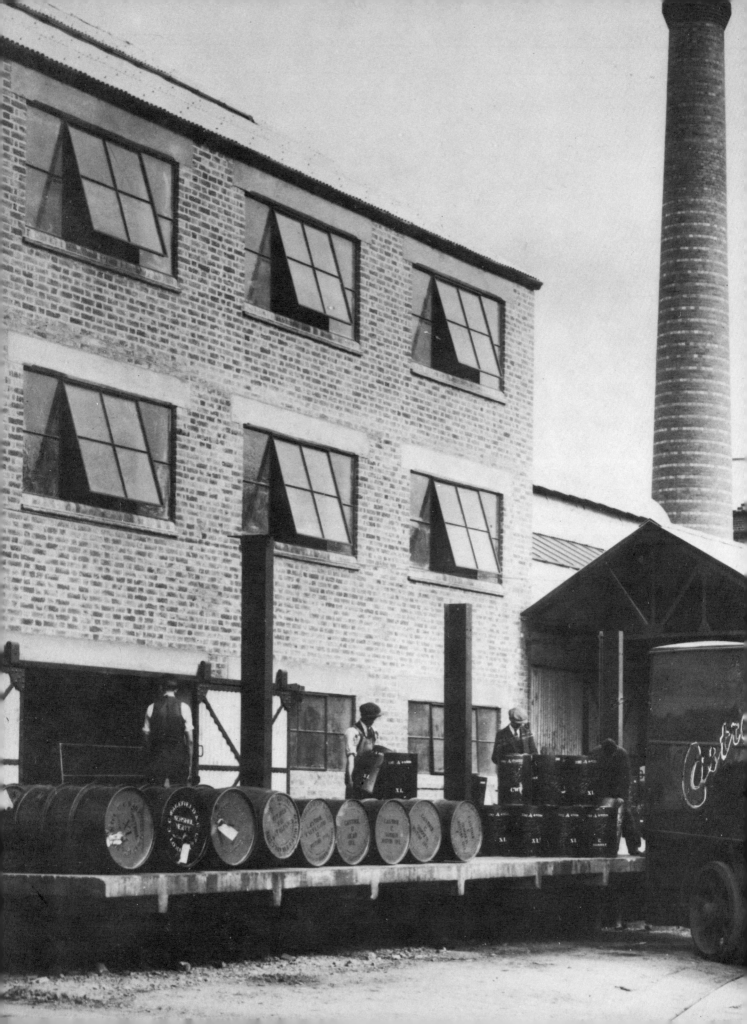

31. An overhead view of one of the last steamers before the remnants of this side of the business were transferred to Atkinson in 1926. The postwar wagons had cross water-tube boilers and 38 hp duplex high-pressure engines in place of the earlier vertical firetube boilers and compound engines.

32. Most of the big names in transport or own-account haulage ran Leylands. Here we see part of J. Lyon's fleet in the mid 1920s with RAF types on the right and newer three tonners on the left. Leyland's association with familiar names led to a famous series of 'slogans we share' advertisements. For example, they borrowed Ovaltine Rusks' catch phrase 'no more teething troubles'.

33. The RAF type was still listed by Leyland in 1925, although by this time the GH type had largely taken its place. The latter was for four ton loads and had a very similar mechanical specification to its illustrious sister. A five ton version was known as the PH and above that came the QH six tonner.

34. Before we leave the famous RAF type behind, let us take a look at a few of the strange things done to it to modernise the design or increase payload. The artic is an Eagle conversion, the Dr. Cassel and Samuel Jones lorries have been converted to pneumatic tyres at the front, and box van 259 has them all round in the 1930s. The lifted bonnet reveals a typical 1930s substitution of a Gardner diesel, whilst the Loblaw artic in Canada has been fitted with a Mercedes-Benz four-cylinder diesel. The original petrol engines were almost impossible to wear out, but very slow. Many were still in use in the 1950s.

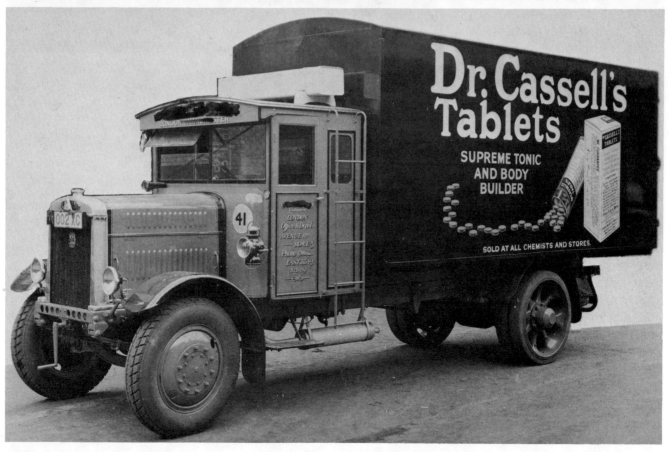

35. A side type SQ2 six tonner of the mid 1920s had a 36 or 40 hp four-cylinder petrol engine. It is amazing to think of this vehicle being driven on the London-Birmingham-Manchester-Liverpool trunk route at the 12 mph legal speed of the time.

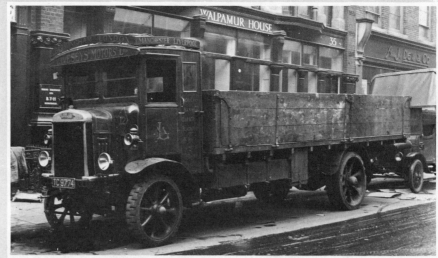

36. A rather novel Bonallack metal cab, designed to permit the carriage of long girders. Note that 20 mph was permitted on pneumatic tyres.

In 1926 Leyland recruited a new chief engineer, G.J. Rackham, who had been with AEC in its early days and with GMC's Yellow Coach subsidiary in America since the First World War. He was responsible for the famous six-cylinder Titan and Tiger buses of late 1927 and for the next generation of lorries that first appeared in late 1928 (when he returned to AEC).

37. In 1927 Leyland built one of the first practical heavy six wheelers. Rigid sixes had been around in Britain since 1923 but were mostly employed for light off-road duties. The SWQ2 was for ten ton loads and had a non-powered centre axle with only single tyres to reduce scrub. A 36 hp engine was normally used, which must have had to work hard when the lorry was fully loaded.

38. In 1928 Leyland returned to the military field with the 6 x 4 three ton capacity 36 hp Terrier. It had an auxiliary gearbox and WD-pattern trunnion-mounted rear suspension with worm driven axles. Many were supplied for arduous civilian service in the colonies and larger and forward-control versions were soon offered. An eight-wheel drive prototype was made soon afterwards but series production was not undertaken.

39. Under general manager A.A. Liardet the Leyland factories were back on full time and profitable operation by the late 1920s. In 1928 came the first of the named truck range, the 2$^{1}/_{2}$ ton TA series Badger and 3$^{1}/_{2}$ ton TC series Beaver. They had Dewandre four-wheel servo brakes, worm drive axles and new ohv four-cylinder engines. This one is a 30 hp Badger with an enamel badge depicting the animal (usually only the bus models went in for this practice). From 1932 the Badger grew into a four tonner and the Beaver became a five tonner.

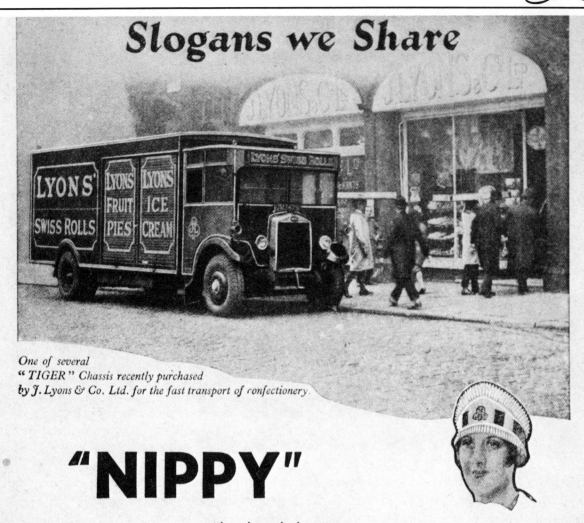

40. The six-cylinder Tiger bus chassis had arrived in 1927 and a few were used for haulage purposes where speed, soft suspension and a low-loading height were important. The shared slogan in this 1930 advertisement refers to the nickname for Lyons' waitresses.

35

41. This SQ2 on pneumatics was photographed by AEC when it delivered Sankey wheels to them at Southall. One wonders why. Perhaps it was for industrial espionage or to use as evidence against Sankey for delivering by rival lorry! Another explanation could lie in the merger talks that are known to have taken place around 1930, though in that case one would have expected the latest Bison, Buffalo or Bull to have created more interest.

42. An SQ2 removal van with 'experienced men'. They were photographed outside a transport café on the London-Postsmouth road. Their prints were no doubt forgotten long ago but this one survived on the café wall until rescued by Arthur Johnson shortly before the building was demolished recently, for road widening.

Leyland **After Two Years' Tests**

in the hands of ordinary users as well as of experts the complete range of the New Heavy-Goods Models is now in full production.

90 cwt. BISON

TG 1	Body space	14'6" × 7'2"
TG 2 Tip	,, ,,	13'6" × 7'0"
TSG 1	,, ,,	17'6" × 7'2"

6 ton BUFFALO

TQ 1	Body space 16'6" × 7'0"

6-7 ton BULL

TSQ 1	Body space	17'6" × 7'2"
TSQ 2 Tip	,,	16'0" × 7'0"
TSQ 3	,, ,,	20'0" × 7'2"

10-12 ton HIPPO

TSW 1	Body space	22'0" × 7'2"
TSW 2 Tip	,, ,,	20'0" × 7'0"

43. In 1929 Leyland took the unusual step of arranging for 3,000 employees to visit Ostend and the First World War battlefields of Flanders. It was the largest works outing up to that date and marked the firm's total recovery from the aftermath of war. More new goods models arrived in Leyland's 'menagerie' of animal names during the year and, as this May 1930 advertisement shows, were soon in full production.

44. A and B. The Bull was classified as a 7^1/$_4$ tonner and was only listed to 1934. Here we have a Lyons 'daylight talkie' publicity van and one fitted with a third axle to increase payload to 12 tons. The Bull was normally intended for trailer work and was fitted with a double reduction axle and a six-cylinder 43.5 hp engine as used in the Titan bus.

45. A and B. Illustrated here is a 1930 Bison with 1100 gallon four compartment petrol tank and special cab incorporating a fire shield. The Bison started as a 4^1/$_2$ tonner, though was rated as a six tonner in the following year. It was also available in TSG form with forward control, as the milk lorry shows. It had four-wheel servo brakes and a four-cylinder 5.9 litre 73 bhp ohv petrol engine.

46. The four- and six-cylinder ohv petrol engines were beautifully made, very sweet running and quiet. The 1935 six-cylinder type shown here came in $4^1/2$ x $5^1/2$ or $4^9/16$ x $5^1/2$ inch bore and stroke versions with capacities of 7.67 and 8.84 litres (468 and 539 cu. ins) and there were four-cylinder types with similar bore and stroke to allow interchangeability of parts. A nice feature of all these engines was the safety starting handle, which did not reverse if the engine back-fired. The whole T series 'zoo' used as many common components as possible.

47. The Beaver rapidly grew up from being the 3¹/₂ tonner announced in 1928. This is a 1933 six-cylinder Beaver with 62 bhp petrol engine, worm or bevel driven axle, servo brakes, four-speed gearbox with 'silent' third, and a load capacity of eight tons including bodyweight. Typical of the careful attention given to mechanical matters was the removable felt oil filter in the under-radiator cooler and the starter ring that could be unbolted and moved round the flywheel to equalise wear. At the end of 1933 the model name was moved from the side (page 40) to the centre bottom of the radiator, exemplified by this trailer-towing vehicle in the 1940s.

48. Though Lynx was later to become a familiar Leyland model name, it was first applied in 1930 by trailer maker Carrimore Six Wheelers Ltd., to an articulated outfit. It used a 100 bhp six-cylinder Leyland engine and could carry about 18 tons. There were servo brakes on all axles (two on the four-in-line rear arrangement) and one operator expressed delight in getting from London to Manchester and back in just over two days, laden both ways.

49. Special short wheelbase petrol tank versions of several models were made but low-frame passenger chassis continued to be popular. Their long wheelbase and low centre of gravity contributed to safety. This is a 1932 1500 gallon Butterfield tanker making extensive use of aluminium alloy. It is based on a Lioness coach chassis with six-cylinder 36/42 hp petrol engine. A larger bus-based Llama 43.5 hp 7$^{1}/_{4}$ tonner was also offered.

50. A and B. The 'zoo' became increasingly complicated with forward- and normal-control versions available for most models and enlarged load capacities. This is a six/seven ton TSQ Bull, which was closely related to the TQ six ton Buffalo. The trailing axle six wheeler is probably a conversion of the same type and not a true Hippo. The latter is shown when still in use in 1949.

51. Having sold its Trojan division in 1928, Leyland needed something else to occupy the 1600 men at their Kingston-on-Thames factory. A mass-produced lightweight two tonner with six-cylinder Chrysler-inspired petrol engine was developed. The Cub appeared in 1930 and entered full production in Spring 1931. This example was employed in the textile trade.

52. Having already seen a forward-control Beaver we now have a fine example of a normal-control six tonner plus trailer. Engines available were four- or six-cylinder petrol or (from 1933) diesel types of 5.7 or 8 litres. The matchboard bodywork is typical of constructional methods of the time.

53. In late 1931 a forward-control version of the Cub was added, with bus, goods and fire appliance variants being manufactured. Unfortunately for the high quality Leyland, cheaper competing Bedfords had now entered the field and sales did not live up to expectations. This was in spite of the range being sold through a separate and larger dealer network than the traditional Leyland 'heavies'.

54. Late in 1933 the Cub stole a march on all its lightweight rivals by offering an in-house diesel option (of the mass-producers, Commer alone had made diesels available and these were bought in from Perkins). The original 27.3 hp petrol engine had developed 60 bhp and the 4.4 litre Light Six diesel had identical output but at 2400 rpm instead of 2000 rpm. It also shared many common components with the petrol engine. In 1932 an 18.2 hp four-cylinder 40 bhp petrol engine option had been added for municipal and local operation. After five years of development, big diesels were introduced to the Leyland range in 1931, initially in the Rhino 12 ton six wheeler, but by 1933 they were being offered for most models.

"The Leyland—she's a Lady"

1 TUESDAY JANUARY

LEYLAND MOTORS Lᵗᵈ. LEYLAND LANCS.

55. A and B. These famous clocks appeared beside the major trunk roads in the 1930s as part of a very successful image-building exercise that included the slogan 'the Leyland, she's a Lady'. This was used in a very popular calendar series showing pretty and refined ladies rather than Leylands. The last clock the author remembers in situ was in Hampshire in the 1960s, admittedly by then swamped in ivy. The example shown here may have been the same one as it was photographed when new by Thornycroft, presumably somewhere near its Basingstoke factory. Another way of keeping in touch with operators and encouraging good relations, was the house magazine the Leyland Journal, which commenced publication in 1935.

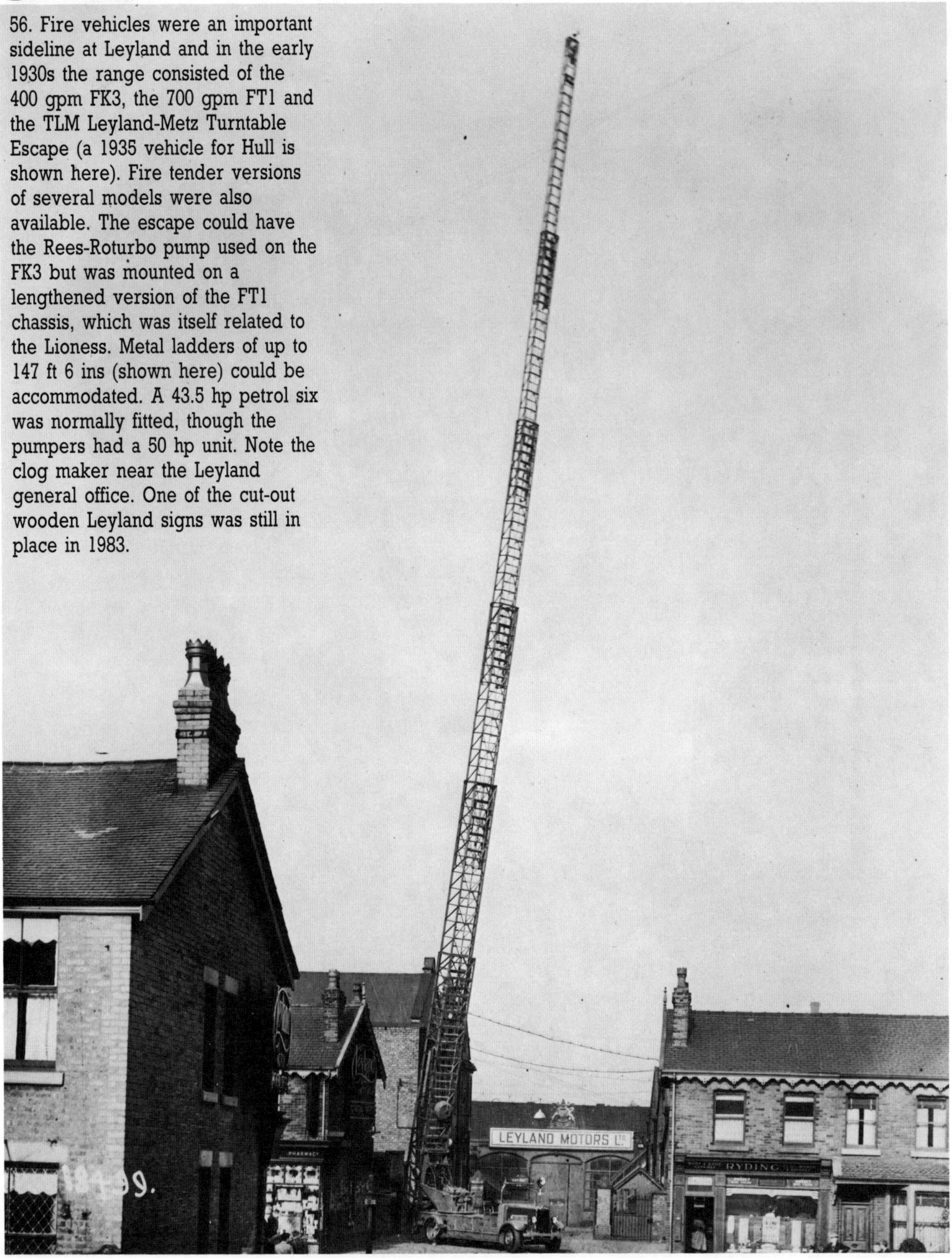

56. Fire vehicles were an important sideline at Leyland and in the early 1930s the range consisted of the 400 gpm FK3, the 700 gpm FT1 and the TLM Leyland-Metz Turntable Escape (a 1935 vehicle for Hull is shown here). Fire tender versions of several models were also available. The escape could have the Rees-Roturbo pump used on the FK3 but was mounted on a lengthened version of the FT1 chassis, which was itself related to the Lioness. Metal ladders of up to 147 ft 6 ins (shown here) could be accommodated. A 43.5 hp petrol six was normally fitted, though the pumpers had a 50 hp unit. Note the clog maker near the Leyland general office. One of the cut-out wooden Leyland signs was still in place in 1983.

57. One of the most popular of the new models that came out in late 1929 was the 12¹/₂ ton payload Hippo. Leyland offered a 6 x 2 with bevel double reduction or 6 x 4 with worm drive, and the 50 hp petrol engine gave a top speed of 35 mph. The 8.4 litre 90 bhp diesel unit was fitted to most from the early 1930s, but this example dating from April 1930 has the petrol engine provided before the diesel became available.

58. We have already encountered a forward-control Beaver and now present a selection of normal-control types (left and overleaf). The Beaver name covered a wide range of six to eight ton models with four- or six-cylinder petrol (33.3 or 43.5 hp) or diesel (32.4 or 48.6 hp) engines. The one on the Welsh hill track is in an army test, the Eagle 1000 gallon cesspool emptier is destined for Poland, the artic is a later 1938 example and the drawbar outfit has Eagle trailer and bodywork.

59.A. This is a Hippo trailing axle chassis with the double reduction, bevel drive axle. A single-spring bogie was used with torque arm on the rear axle. There were triple Dewandre servos and a four-speed gearbox with separate step-up box on the centre cross-member. This was arranged to give a fifth gear rather than double all the ratios in the main box. An autovac on the bulkhead drew up fuel.

59.B. The detail shows the patented handbrake arrangement used on most contemporary Leyland models which was developed initially for the Terrier. It could hold a laden vehicle on a 1 in 4 hill.

60. Though the Badger was typically of normal-control layout this photograph shows a forward-control version in 1933. This is actually an ultra-short conversion with front axle set a foot behind the normal position. It had a 28.9 hp four-cylinder ohv petrol engine and carried four ton loads of paper from London Docks to Fleet Street. The wheelbase was only 9ft 6ins.

61.A, B and C. A three axle version of the Cub was developed in 1931. It had balancer-beam rear suspension in which the rear axle was on trailing arms, the forward ends of which acted as the rear shackle point for the springs of the leading axle. Because of the geometry of the arms the rear wheels took a third less weight than the driving wheels. As well as the chassis, tanker and van versions are illustrated here and overleaf.

62. A and B. In 1935 the Z type second series pushrod ohv Cub engine arrived, making the petrol and diesel versions even more similar. They were of 4.7 litres capacity and developed 85 and 71 bhp respectively. With this engine came the change of styling shown on the Titus Ward van in contrast to the more delicate traditional pattern exemplified by the 1933 two ton Haig van.

63. A 10 ft wheelbase forward-control Cub with four-cylinder petrol engine developing 40 bhp was available from 1932. The Derby-type body held seven cubic yards of refuse. Watford coil ignition was standard though a magneto could be specified. Top speed at 3000 rpm was 40 mph.

64. The first production Leyland diesels were offered in the bonneted Rhino six wheeler in late 1931. This shows the installation and a complete view of a similar 8.1 litre 90 bhp engine of the following year with revised manifolding and auxiliaries. Towards the end of 1933 capacity was increased to 8.6 litres. Overall dimensions were comparable with the petrol units. The diesels had direct injection and ohv and required no glow plugs for starting.

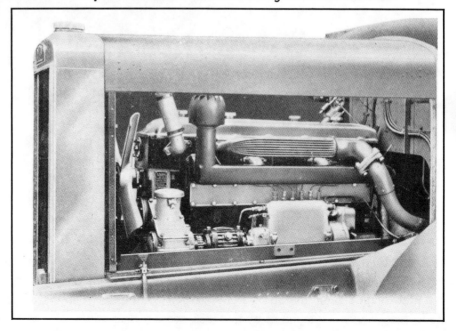

65. An interesting short wheelbase Badger with Eagle tower and crew body. The 'Gearless' designation on the radiator shows that this is one of the few lorries fitted with the Lysholm-Smith torque converter that Leyland developed from 1931 and offered from 1933. It was best known on the Gearless Tiger bus, of which 2000 were sold in five years. The transmission contained centrifugal pump, driven rotor and outer casing with stator blades. The liquid used for the hydraulic medium was paraffin mixed with fuel oil. The converter gave smooth progress to 20 mph and allowed 1 in 5 hills to be climbed.

66. About 8000 Cubs were built and competition in the lightweight class was so fierce that towards the end of its production run increasingly large versions were offered. In 1936 came this double-drive example with a capacity of six tons (1200 gallons plus tank). Though this weight could have readily been carried on a two axle truck the petrol companies in certain situations preferred the greater stability and traction available with 6 x 4.

67. The Cub bus (latterly in rear-engined form) and goods range lasted to 1940, one of the final variants being a fire appliance. The name was revived much later on passenger chassis. Before leaving it and considering its close relative, the Lynx, here is a selection of late Z types. They include a 6 x 4 six ton chassis with two-spring bogie; a KZ5 six ton artic, a pair of three ton vans and catalogue extract showing that many could be kept under $2\frac{1}{2}$ tons unladen weight and be allowed to travel at 30 mph. The 50 per cent power increase refers to the Z engine that produced 85 bhp mentioned earlier. (below and overleaf)

THE NEW *Leyland*

CUB

3·6 TON RANGE

Leyland Motors Ltd

with 30 M.P.H. MODELS and 50% GREATER POWER

68. A and B. New to Croydon in 1936 was this 100 ft Metz escape with 500 gpm pump. Leyland held British Empire rights to the German design which incorporated an automatic plumbing arrangement to keep the ladder upright, even if the chassis should tilt up to ten degrees sideways. The machine is shown here prior to delivery and was to remain in service for 30 years before eventual purchase for preservation. Similar machines were supplied all over the world, including several to Buenos Aires with 132 ft ladders.

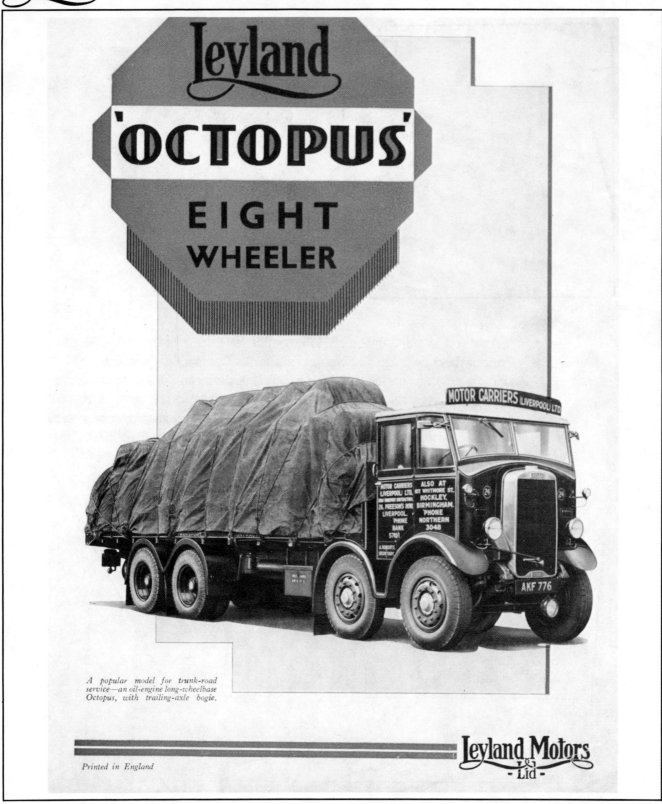

A popular model for trunk-road service—an oil-engine long-wheelbase Octopus, with trailing-axle bogie.

Printed in England

69. Late in 1934 came the famous Octopus eight wheeler, illustrated on the front cover of a November 1935 sales leaflet. Diesel or petrol engines of just under 50 hp rating were available and drive was offered on the first or both rear axles. A four-speed gearbox was deemed adequate to begin with, but a new five-speed box was soon available. Gross vehicle weight was 22 tons.

70. A version of the Cub was extensively revised to take better advantage of 2½ ton, 30 mph and £30 tax concession in 1937. It had semi-forward control and was known as the Lynx. Its engine was identical to the Cub's except for the new aluminium cylinder head. With a very skimpy platform body it could carry six tons, though five tons was more typical.

71.A & B. A handsome Sparshatt bodied Lynx and a typical chassis drawing (overleaf) supplied to coachbuilders by Leyland, showing a shorter 10 ft 3 ins wheelbase type. As well as giving dimensions, the drawing specified items that had to be left clear like lubricators and the fuel filler. Leyland also offered complete factory-built Lynx trucks from Kingston.

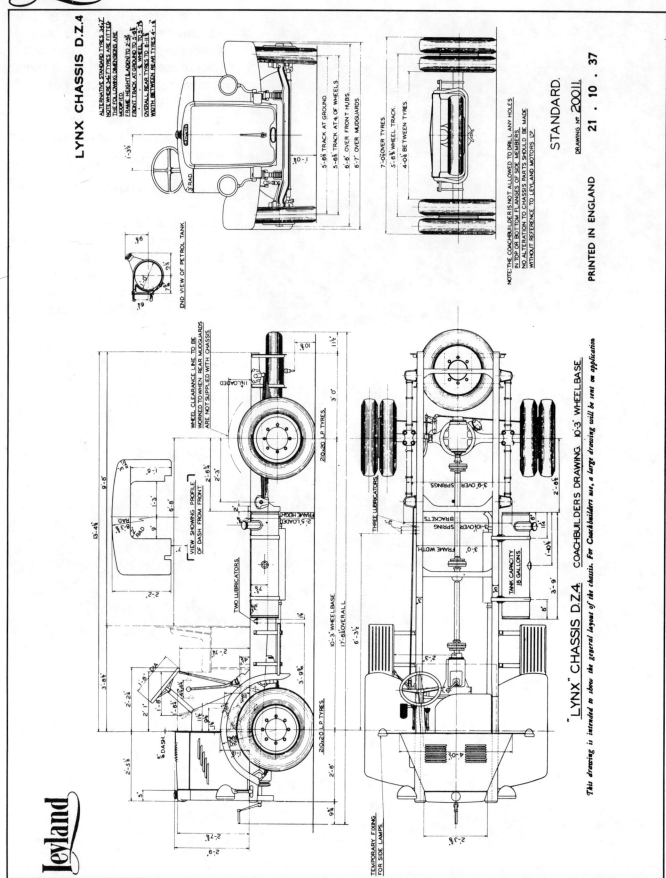

LYNX CHASSIS D.Z.4

ALTERNATIVE STANDARD TYRES 34·7.
NOTE WHERE 34·7 TYRES ARE FITTED
THE FOLLOWING DIMENSIONS ARE
MODIFIED.
FRAME HEIGHT & GROUND TO 2·5¼
FRONT TRACK AT GROUND 5·6⅝
" " & WHEEL TO 5·6¾
OVERALL REAR TYRES TO 6·11⅝
WIDTH BETWEEN REAR TYRES 4·1⅛

STANDARD.

DRAWING Nᵒ 20011.

21 . 10 . 37

PRINTED IN ENGLAND

NOTE: THE COACHBUILDER IS NOT ALLOWED TO DRILL ANY HOLES
IN TOP OR BOTTOM FLANGES OF SIDE MEMBERS.
NO ALTERATION TO CHASSIS PARTS SHOULD BE MADE
WITHOUT REFERENCE TO LEYLAND MOTORS LTᵈ

"LYNX" CHASSIS D.Z.4.   COACHBUILDER'S DRAWING.   10·3" WHEELBASE.

This drawing is intended to show the general layout of the chassis. For Coachbuilders use, a large drawing will be sent on application

END VIEW OF PETROL TANK

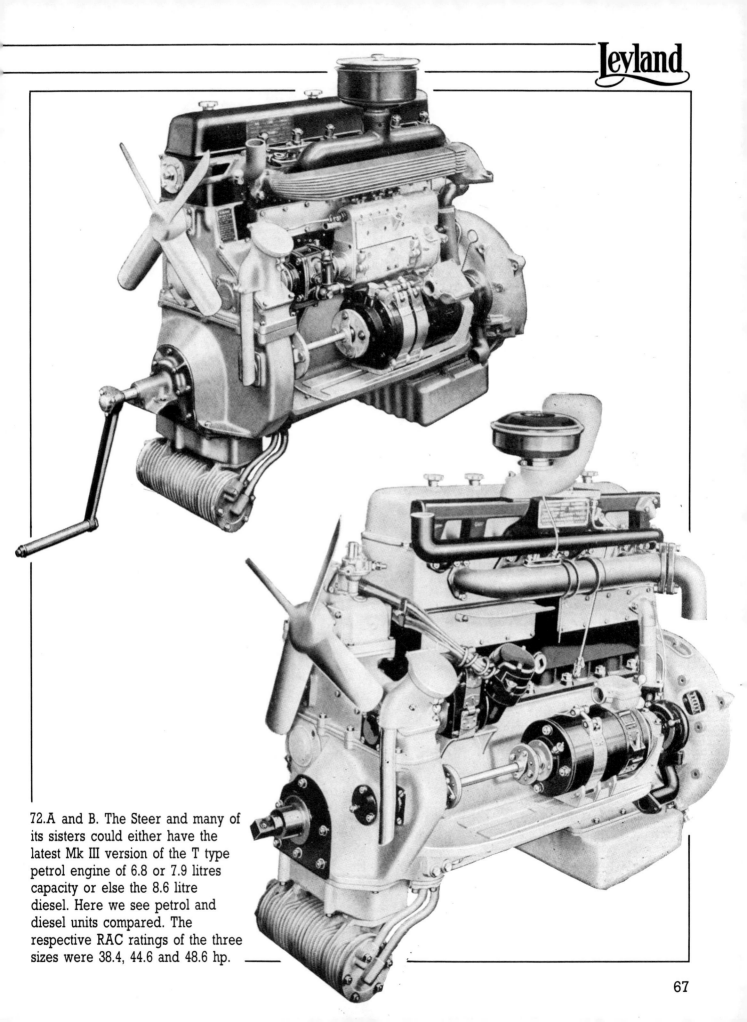

Leyland

72.A and B. The Steer and many of its sisters could either have the latest Mk III version of the T type petrol engine of 6.8 or 7.9 litres capacity or else the 8.6 litre diesel. Here we see petrol and diesel units compared. The respective RAC ratings of the three sizes were 38.4, 44.6 and 48.6 hp.

Leaflet No. 548A

Leyland

'STEER'

SIX-CYLINDER
TWIN-STEERED
HEAVY-DUTY
GOODS CHASSIS

Equal tyre loading is a feature of the Steer

Printed in England

Leyland Motors
- L&J Ltd -

The "Steer"—a vehicle with a platform length of 20' 6"
and a payload capacity of over 10 tons

73.A & B. These two Steer catalogues make an interesting contrast because the artist's impression of the streamlined version is depicted for the 1937 model, whereas a year later the traditional type is shown. Based on the Beaver (indeed the model was originally called a Twin Steer Beaver), they had bevel double reduction or worm rear axles. The five-speed gearbox was standard and $10^{1}/4$ tons could be carried, plus $6^{1}/2$ tons of trailer and load.

THE **Leyland** 'BEAVER' **4** 4-CYLINDER 6/8-TONNER

One of the Beaver Fours in the service of a well-known gravel company

Printed in England.

Leyland Motors Ltd

74. This 1935 Beaver Four (indicating four-cylinder 32.4 hp diesel or 33.3 hp petrol engines) was for six to eight ton loads depending on bodywork. The type had worm drive, four-speed gearboxes, and forward or normal control. As on other contemporary Leylands, the front wheel brake servos followed the angle of the wheels when being steered.

75. A 1939 Limousine pumper with wheeled escape shown in the 1960s when at the end of its service life. Enclosed bodies were adopted by many brigades early in the 1930s and examples were built on Cub, six wheel Terrier, and Lioness types. Leyland also did much to persuade brigades to purchase diesel appliances in the later 1930s.

76. One of the last peacetime Beavers, provided with an alloy body by W. H. Goddard of Oadby. The Farington site received a new 3½ acre engine shop with £200,000 worth of machine tools just before the war to double output. Alongside it an axle shop was built to cater for both Lancashire- and Surrey-built Leylands.

77. During the war a three tonner development of the Terrier called the Retriever was built at the rate of about fifty per week. It had a 5.9 litre 73 bhp four-cylinder petrol engine and these vehicles found use as GS wagons, workshops, mobile cranes, and wireless vans, amongst many other duties. 6542 were eventually produced.

A tank factory was established alongside the Farington complex and, as well as working on several other machines, Leyland designed and produced the complete Comet tank at Kingston.

78. About 1500 Lynx were built at Kingston during the second World War. This is a 1941 example that was used to carry 'pool' petrol.

The Leyland payroll grew to nearly 11 000 during the war and produced some 3000 tanks, 10 000 tank engines, about 10 000 wheeled vehicles, pumping sets (from the fire vehicle factory at Chorley), as well as castings and millions of shells.

79. A Mk I Hippo with the Pool Board. Production ended when tank development took precedence, but late in 1943 a Mk II diesel 101 bhp version could be accommodated and about 1000 were made up to the war's end. Other six wheelers included over 300 Beaver-Eels, which were semi-armoured vehicles carrying anti-aircraft guns for defending aircraft factories.

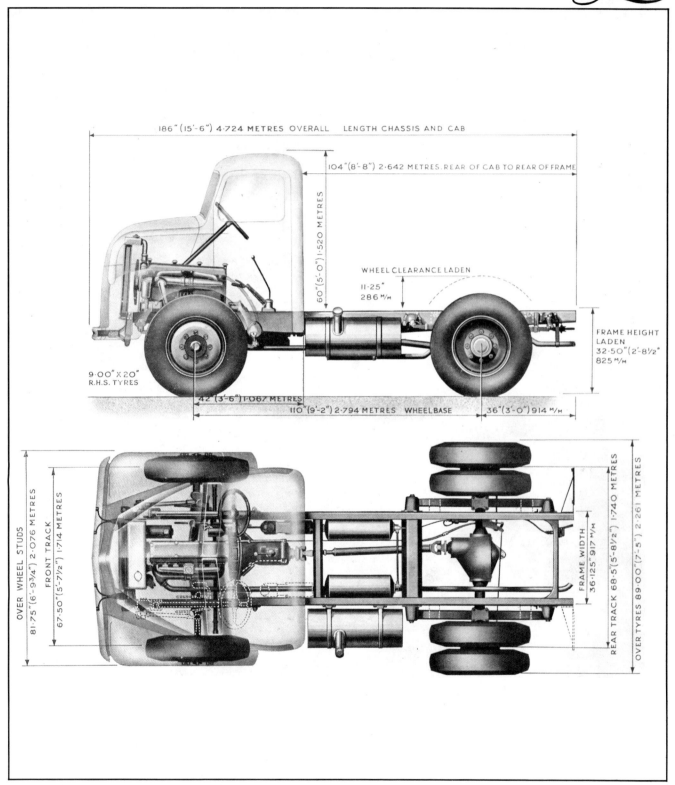

186" (15'-6") 4·724 METRES OVERALL   LENGTH CHASSIS AND CAB

104" (8'-8") 2·642 METRES. REAR OF CAB TO REAR OF FRAME

60"(5'-0") 1·520 METRES

WHEEL CLEARANCE LADEN

11·25"
286 M/M

FRAME HEIGHT
LADEN
32·50" (2'-8½")
825 M/M

9·00" X 20"
R.H.S. TYRES

42" (3'-6") 1·067 METRES

110" (9'-2") 2·794 METRES WHEELBASE

36" (3'-0") 914 M/M

OVER WHEEL STUDS
81·75" (6'-9¾") 2·076 METRES

FRONT TRACK
67·50" (5'-7½") 1·714 METRES

REAR TRACK 68·5" (5'-8½") 1·740 METRES

FRAME WIDTH
36·125" 917 M/M

OVER TYRES 89·00" (7'-5") 2·261 METRES

80. At the end of 1946 Leyland's workforce numbered 9000 (compared with 6000 ten years earlier) and its vastly expanded factories were returning to civilian output. Buses and lorries were needed to replace ageing and destroyed fleets but, most of all, Britain needed foreign currency. Leyland, whose export record before the war had been good, decided to produce a 'world truck' in 1947, named after its Comet tank. Here we see a 'ghosted' tractive unit.

81.A and B. A 1951 Comet articulated tanker and 1953 tipper showing the spectacular transatlantic styling that made them popular in Britain and in many territories that had bought American vehicles in the past. It was a natural successor to the Lynx in both petrol (100 bhp) and diesel (75 bhp) versions. The engines once again used many interchangeable parts and were of 5.08 litres capacity (306 cu. ins and therefore designated 0.300, as opposed to the 0.600 used in heavy models from 1946). They had five-speed gearboxes and bevel rear axles.

82. Over 5000 trucks and buses were built in 1948, and in 1949 exports showed an increase of 21.5 per cent over the previous year and accounted for 42 per cent of the 6291 total output. As part of the sales drive, standard printing blocks were supplied to agents around the world for their letterheads and advertising. This is a 125 bhp Super Beaver intended for Spanish-speaking areas and sporting a badge proclaiming 'El Camion Inglese'.

83. A new metal cab with enclosed grille was developed immediately after the war and here we see a 1948 example on a Hippo with 125 bhp 0.600 diesel. It has a Pilot body and tipping gear and was used for coke haulage. The same cab was used on forward-control versions of the Comet and many of the heavyweights.

84. 1950 was an important year for Leyland. 35 years old Donald Stokes, who had joined as an apprentice in 1930, became high-flying sales manager, and moving track assembly was adopted at Farington (by this time Kingston was no longer producing trucks). Then in 1951 the Chorley spares operation started and Albion was taken over. Meanwhile, trucks continued to be supplied for all manner of duties, one of the most unusual being the conversion of Beavers by Auto-Mowers into winch trucks for forestry work or petroleum exploration.

85. A 1952 advertisement showing the three standard types of cab offered and Hippo, Beaver and Comet chassis. A special military chassis, the 6 x 6 Martian, was made available at this time. It had a four-speed synchromesh gearbox with three-speed transfer box. Following the acquisition of Scammell in 1955, the need for Leyland themselves to produce such 'specials' was diminished.

86. A 1947 Octopus 22 ton gvw tanker looking very austere without the wing embellishments that were soon adopted on the front apron. The other views show the evolution of the cab styling through the 1940s and then the horizontal grille adopted in the early 1950s.

87.A. In 1949 the 0.300 was joined by the 0.350 followed by the 0.375 shown here in section. The primary difference between the two larger types was bore dimension. The 0.350 was fitted to the Comet 90 (bhp) which in the mid 1950s grew to 100 bhp. The 0.375 was used in 110 bhp versions, particularly those used for articulated operation.

87.B. In 1950 Thompson Bros (Bilston) Ltd produced the largest rigid aircraft refueller of its day. It was of unitary chassisless construction and had a capacity of 4000 gallons. Leyland 0.600 diesel and running gear were used. It had a gvw of almost 26 tons, a length of 30 ft, and could accommodate six in its cab, from which there was a ladder exit to the tank top. Other versions were built as twin-steer six wheelers. 400 gpm pumping equipment was installed and here we see an example beside a DC4 — the latter known as an Argonaut when powered by Rolls-Royce Merlin engines, as here. In 1969 Thompson produced an Octopus-based 9000 gallon refueller which grossed 95 tons with 11 000 gallon trailer.

88. Henry Spurrier Junior was still leading the company in 1955 and was knighted in that year. The Spurrier works, the largest tank factory in Europe, was acquired from the government at the end of the Korean War to boost Leyland output. Meanwhile the forward-control Comet continued to sell well at home. Here is a 1954 Comet 90 for 7$\frac{1}{2}$ ton loads.

89.A. The Hippo II military-type chassis remained in production for a time after the war and ex-War Department types were also plentiful. They were used for all manner of heavy-duty work including skid loading 15 tons of oilfield equipment in the Dutch East Indies in the early 1950s. Here we have one in 1959 equipped with a German Kässbohrer tower crane.

89.B & C. From the 1920s Leyland had a Canadian sales and assembly plant which at various times made specific models for local requirements, including this 1928 Lioness for beer delivery in Toronto. In the early 1950s it offered normal-control trucks, using the Briggs cab of the Comet, a longer hood (bonnet) and US-type grille. Then in 1956 came a small series using the International cab shown here. Production ended two years later. Leyland was involved with the Cancar bus firm (who built the final trucks) and with Hayes, who were British Columbia agents from the 1930s and used Leyland components in some of their own trucks.

90. The Comet was a useful basis for specialist conversions as it was competitively priced yet of superior quality to the average mass-produced chassis. Douglas used Comet parts in many of its aircraft tugs and also made this 6 x 4 truck chassis in 1954 using its own single-leaf spring, trunnion-mounted bogie. With auxiliary gearbox in low-low it could climb a 1 in 2.5 hill with ten tons aboard.

91. A 1954 Beaver flat truck with demountable livestock body in service in Scotland. It could carry over six tons and had the 125 bhp, 9.8 litre 0.600 five-speed constant mesh gearbox, overhead worm axle and air brakes (unlike the vacuum hydraulic type fitted to the contemporary Comet).

92. The 0.680 was an 11.1 litre version of the 0.600 engine which was first used in horizontal form in tthe Royal Tiger Worldmaster psv of the mid 1950s. It moved into the heaviest truck models in 200 bhp vertical form in the early 1960s. Here we have an unusual turbocharged version with Cromard cylinder liners and 240 bhp output.

Engine production moved into the 100 acre Spurrier works and by 1959 117,000 diesels had been made since the war and were being added to at the rate of 750 per week. As well as numerous industrial and plant users the following British vehicle makers offered Leyland power at the time: Douglas, Rowe, Aveling-Barford, Euclid, Guy, Seddon, Albion and Scammell. There were numerous overseas licence-holding producers, who included DAF, Pegaso, Ashok, OAF, Sisu and several factories in Iron Curtain countries.

93.A and B. From 1956 All Wheel Drive Ltd of Camberley made 4 x 4 versions of the 0.350 engined Comet that could climb 30 degree slopes with five tons aboard. Here we see one equipped with Failing oilfield equipment and another being put through its paces at Chobham FVRDE testing ground.

CANNED FRUITS. VEGETABLES. PRESERVES.

STRATFORD ON AVON

PRODUCE CANNERS LTD

SonA

94. More in keeping with the late 1930s (when Chas. A. Wells ran a very similar Octopus) than the early 1950s was this magnificent Octopus van with highly imaginative sign writing and layout. Unfortunately the colour scheme and bodybuilder are not recorded. Rigid eight vans with Luton heads, which were never a common sight, went under the colloquial name of showboats.

95. A wartime Merryweather-equipped Leyland wages war on pigeons in later life. It is shown in New Palace Yard, Westminster, being used to reach difficult ledges, where sticky paste was spread to discourage roosting. In 1965 an even earlier 1938 Leyland-Metz was sent to Paris by Rentokil for similar purposes.

96. In 1958 Leyland shared tooling and development costs with Dodge in Motor Panels' LAD (Leyland-Albion-Dodge) all-steel cab. Leyland called it their Vista-Vue and gradually fitted it to all their forward-control models. This is a 1959 Super Comet nine tonner with 110 bhp 0.375 diesel. In the following year the engine range was modified and called the Power-Plus series, those used in Comets then becoming 0.370 and 0.400 of 110 and 125 bhp — outputs previously achieved with larger engines. The Power-Plus was four to ten per cent more economical and had a 12 000 hour life expectancy between major overhauls.

97.A. A sectioned view of the new Vista-Vue. This is a 1961 Super Comet tractive unit with 0.400 Power-Plus engine. The pressed steel cab frame was clothed in pressed steel panels, although fibreglass panels were briefly offered from 1960. To enable the engine to be taken out, the grille and bumper were removed and the engine unbolted and slid through the aperture.

In 1961 Leyland gained some smaller vehicles with the acquisition of Standard-Triumph and in the following year the AEC Thornycroft, Maudslay, Crossley empire was added.

Leyland

20 YEARS OLD...

500,000 MILES SO FAR...

GOOD FOR THOUSANDS MORE

RICHARD BIFFA LIMITED

CONTRACTORS TO GOVERNMENT DEPARTMENTS AND LOCAL AUTHORITIES. SAND AND BALLAST MERCHANTS. HARDCORE, ASHES AND CLINKER. CONTRACT AND DAILY HIRE. PLANT HIRE. RUBBISH CLEARANCE AND EXCAVATION.

YOUR REF

OUR REF PAK/GPD

WEMBLEY HILL ROAD,
WEMBLEY, MIDDLESEX

Telephone: WEMbley 4334/5/6   (3 lines)

Directors:
L. G. BIFFA
D. G. BIFFA
R. F. BIFFA

Secretary:
P. R. HIGGS

Messrs. Leyland Motors Limited,   6th July, 1959
Leyland,
Lancs.

Dear Sirs,

    For the last eighteen months we have been carrying out a large haulage contract clearing approximately 200,000 tons of excavated material from the South East London Area, the bulk of the cartage being dealt with by Leyland 'Hippos'. We would like to say right away that we are completely satisfied at the performance of these trucks. Working in the appalling conditions of last winter (and summer) they steadfastly shifted some 144 to 156 cubic yards per vehicle per day. They have been working at full stretch six days a week and although there may have been an odd spring breakage here and there, we have yet to know engine trouble or experience differential, or transmission failure. We are happy to say that the 'Hippo' has proved itself on this class of work; it has the surge of power necessary, and with its double-drive bogie it rarely gets bogged down. Incidentally, two of our 'Hippos' are twenty years old and although they have covered some five hundred thousand miles each they look good for many thousands more.

    Yours faithfully,
p.p. RICHARD BIFFA LIMITED

P. A. King
Manager.

 **HIPPO 6-WHEELER**

20 TONS GROSS

LEYLAND MOTORS LTD., LEYLAND, LANCS. Sales Division: HANOVER HOUSE, HANOVER SQUARE, LONDON, W.1. Tel.: MAYfair 8561

Advertisement published by Leyland Motors Ltd., during the month of April, 1960

97.B & C. A fine testimonial to the longevity of the 0.600 engine and Leyland design and construction in general in an advertisement published in 1960. The Bristol Freighter was shown in Australia in the late 1960s being loaded with wood from a truck that was nearly forty years old. The original caption referred to the age of the plane but ignored the truck!

98. Power-Plus versions of the 0.600 and 0.680 gave 140 and 200 bhp and were used on the Hippo, Beaver, Octopus, etc. This 200 bhp Octopus worked in a lignite pit in New Zealand. Gross train weight was 38 tons and payload averaged about 25 tons per trip to a refrigeration plant nearby.

99. A 1964 9.8 litre 140 bhp Power-Plus Beaver shown in the year that the Ergomatic tilt cab appeared. However, the fixed Vista-Vue carried on for another fifteen years on Leylands and Albions for rugged service. The Beaver had a spiral bevel axle with hub-reduction and five-speed constant-mesh gearbox with optional overdrive and crawler ratios. The 0.680 engine rated at 225 bhp was available in some versions, notably 35 tonne articulated outfits sold in France by Hotchkiss.

100.A, B, C and D. The heavy-duty bonneted export range continued in the 1960s. The dropside six wheeler 200 bhp Hippo was for use in 30 ton gvw tyre testing in Poland (note the pressure adjusting pipes on the rear bogie). The Buffalo with wrap-round screen is a pre Power-Plus machine of the late 1950s using Leyland's largest engine of 15.2 litres capacity to deliver 200 bhp. Overleaf – the articulated low-loader is shown in 1965 with Dyson trailer for export from Liverpool, and the Super Beaver tipper is in Africa. They had five- or seven-speed gearboxes and hub reduction axles.

101. We have seen that AWD converted various Leyland chassis to 4 x 4. As demand increased in the 1960s it was decided to produce an in-house version of the 4 x 4 Comet. Not surprisingly, in view of their off-road experience, Scammell were entrusted with the development work. Gross weight in arduous use was 9$\frac{1}{2}$ tons and, as can be seen, the cab was raised considerably for increased wheel clearance.

102. As part of their purchase of Standard-Triumph in 1961, Leyland gained the Standard Atlas light commercial vehicle range. This was revised as the Leyland 15 and 20, the smaller 15 cwt capacity version of 1965 being shown. It had a 1670 cc Standard petrol engine, though the 1 ton 20 had choice of 2138 cc petrol or 2260 cc diesel engines. A similar vehicle was modified by Scammell as their Scarab Four. The Leyland merger with BMH (Austin, Morris, Guy, etc.) in 1968 ended the need for the van models.

103.A and B. Apart from the Standard vans Leyland had no small commercials until it launched the 90 (its gross vehicle weight in cwt) in 1962. This used a 2611 cc four-cylinder Standard diesel. The lowered Vista-Vue cab was not a happy styling compromise. The model was built by Standard-Triumph in Coventry and was another type that became surplus to requirements after the merger with BMH. The tidier looking cab was designed for use on Iranian assembled versions.

104. In 1963 Donald Stokes became managing director of the new Leyland Motor Corporation. The Leyland co-founder, Sir Henry Spurrier, was briefly chairman but died in 1964, the year of the Freightline models with Michelotti-styled Ergomatic tilt cabs. Here we have a glimpse of different stages of development, along with some bonneted export trucks. Second from left is a wooden mock-up, whilst the cab to the left was used for testing the ergonomics of the design. The two centre vehicles are the finalised prototypes, with one shown tilted to 55 degrees for engine access.

105. The lighter Beavers and the new Retriever three axle freight and tipper chassis received the Freightline cab first. Heavy-duty trucks, like this 32 ton gtw Hippo, continued to be supplied with the Vista-Vue. This is one of a fleet used with 'jinkers' (pole trailers) in Kaiangarao State Forest, New Zealand.

106. Ashok Motors Ltd started in 1948 by assembling British kits in India. The locally manufactured content of its product soon increased and with financial and technical help from Leyland became the largest heavy truck maker in India. Many of the models it constructed were unique to Ashok, like this 4 x 4 Comet of the early 1960s, using an AWD conversion kit with an earlier style of cab and carrying a Coles mobile crane.

107. The Super Comet received the Ergomatic cab in 1966 and here we have a 10 cu. yd Edbro bodied tipper. Three years later the 55 000th Super Comet was built, nine years from the model's inception. A new 401 version of the 400 engine, producing 138 bhp, was developed for 1969 and gvw of the new truck was 16 tons.

PROVISIONAL *Specification No. 949*

32 TONS G.T.W.

Leyland
STEER
FREIGHTLINE

Over 30 cwt greater capacity than conventional 4-wheel tractors under U.K. regulations

heavy-duty three-axled twin steer tractor chassis with semi-automatic transmission for two-pedal trucking

108. An interesting production trial in 1966 involved fitting pre-selective semi-automatic gearboxes (Leyland had acquired Self-Changing Gears Ltd in 1960). The Steer 32 ton gtw tractive unit used a four-speed version with two-speed axle and 0.680 200 bhp engine. It was based on the two axle Beaver which was available with the same transmission. In actual production a five-speed gearbox with integral splitter was used to give ten ratios.

109. Leyland's factories covered almost 350 acres when this view of a production line was taken in 1966. This is less automated than most because the vehicles involved are 'specials' in the shape of pre-selective, two pedal 32 ton gtw Beavers. A new 140 acre site was bought in 1966 for the construction of a factory to build the new generation of fixed head 500 engines.

110. In late 1968 came the public announcement of operator trials with 38 tonne 370 bhp gas turbine outfits. These had five-speed automatic (Pneumo-cyclic) transmission and received styling and interior treatment from David Bache of Rovers, a company acquired by Leyland in 1966 which had long standing gas turbine experience. Though reliable, their fuel consumption and specialised servicing requirements led to the eventual cancellation of the project.

111.A and B. The Fixed Head 500 six-cylinder diesel that appeared in August 1968 was an ingenious cross-flow design with overhead camshaft and non-detachable cylinder head designed to put an end to gasket problems. It had a capacity of 8.2 litres and developed 170 bhp, or up to 260 bhp when turbocharged. Auxiliaries could be mounted on either side for right – or left-hand drive. Early engines suffered from head cracking due to heat stresses, but it went on to a successful future, particularly in the National bus. The new plant behind the Spurrier general engine factory is shown, containing £$\frac{1}{2}$ million of new machine tools.

112.A, B and C. A revised version of the Ergomatic cab was fitted to the new Fixed Head 500 powered Lynx and Bison late in 1968. It was set five inches higher and had neater frontal styling. The Bison was a 24 ton gvw six wheeler, whilst the Lynx was a 26/28 ton gtw artic machine or 16 ton rigid. A 32 ton artic or drawbar Buffalo or Super Buffalo rigid six, using the same cab and many other components, followed in 1972 and was fitted with a turbocharged version of the engine called the 510. The Buffalos had ten-speed range-change gearboxes and the others had six-speed constant mesh gearboxes.

113.A and B. The traditional style of Ergomatic cab continued for a time on the Beaver and Super Comet. Leylands were exported all over the world, but here we see a 200 bhp Beaver working at 16 256 kg gvw in an unusual setting – Tokyo. Articulated Beavers were available from late 1968 with a 240 bhp turbocharged version of the 0.680 (shown in partially sectioned form) launched in 1966 that was known as the 690 (not to be confused with an AEC power unit with this designation). Lighter versions of the preceding 0.680 powered Beaver with 0.600 engine were known as Badgers.

114. A remarkable machine to European eyes is this Octopus articulated outfit working in New Zealand in the 1960s. The box behind the cab provided both a living compartment and extra load space. Manoeuvrability cannot have been its strong point. The tare weight quoted on the tractive unit is 9-14-1 (tons, cwt and qrs).

115. An unfamiliar Leyland appeared on the front cover of the *Leyland Journal* in 1967. At this time there was an Israeli assembly factory operated by Leyland Ashdod and this was its version of the Super Beaver. The truck was part of a large export order for Peru. Leyland Ashdod operated from 1960 to 1973.

116. The Danish DAB bus factory became a Leyland subsidiary in the 1970s. This car transporter was built by them from an 0.400 engined Tiger Cub psv chassis and carried Saabs from Sweden to Denmark and then Citroëns back to Sweden and Norway. The same chassis was also the basis of half-cab and ultra-low cab transporters in New Zealand and elsewhere.

117. In the mid 1970s the Dutch Leyland sales organisation fitted attractive locally produced cabs to several sizes of Leyland chassis. An unusual feature was that the wiper spindles passed through the windscreen glass. Most carried a Meteeor badge under the radiator grille. In 1970 AEC had acquired a share in the Verhul bus and truck firm in Holland. The firm passed to Leyland, but after 1972 it only made buses.

118.A & B. In a corner of the Ergomatic cab development picture shown earlier a bonneted truck, looking more like a Commer or a Dodge, can be seen. This was an export successor to the old Comet using a proprietary Airflow Streamlines cab and 0.400 Power-Plus engine. 2 000 were ordered for use in Iran at 14 tons gvw. Assembly of a subsequent Super Comet with 401 engine started in Iran in 1969, and for this a Scottish Leyland cab with locally produced bonnet and wings was developed. An example with steel tipping body is shown.

119. In 1968 Leyland merged with the old BMC firm – the latter by this time called British Motor Holdings, as it too had recently taken over other companies, including Jaguar/Daimler/Guy. The Austin and Morris trucks were briefly badged BMC with a Leyland symbol, but then in July 1970 became Bathgate, Scotland, built Leylands. Because of their 'cheap and cheerful' origins they were separated in marketing strategy from the true Leyland 'Bluelines' and were known as 'Redlines'. Here we have a Terrier with a 92 bhp six-cylinder BMC engine and gvw of 19 140 lbs.

120. At one end of the Redline weight scale were Terriers, Boxers, Lairds, etc. (some of which were assembled for the continent at Malines, Belgium, in 1970), but illustrating the other extreme was the Mastiff for 16 tons gvw. It had a Perkins 179 bhp V8 diesel. The tilt cab used on this and sister Bathgate models had originated with BMC in 1964, the year in which the tilt Ergomatic had appeared. Other versions of the Mastiff came as 26-28 ton artic outfits or 22-24 ton six wheelers.

Two axle forward control tipper, haulage and tractor chassis

121. An unusual model shown here in a 1968 catalogue was the Albion-based Super Comet Eland, primarily for South Africa. It retained the Vista-Vue cab long after Comets in Britain had changed to the Ergomatic and used the 401 diesel developing 138 bhp. It had a nine-speed gearbox, Albion hub reduction axle and was for 31 360 lbs gvw on hard roads, or less in arduous conditions.

122. The higher weight limits applied to European roads and the more powerful trucks available there left Leyland with a gap in its range. Operators anticipating an increase from the current 32 tons maximum in Britain (38 tonnes was finally adopted in 1983) and doing international journeys were buying foreign premium heavyweights. Leyland's answer in 1973 was the Marathon, shown here in component form. It used a raised version of the Ergomatic cab and the 273 bhp Leyland TL12 12.47 litre six-cylinder diesel based on an AEC design. The Marathon was initially assembled in the AEC factory, and later at Guy and Scammell. Production of the TL12 engine moved from AEC at Southall to Lancashire.

123. BMC launched their FG cab in 1959. It became known as the 'threepenny bit' because of its angular design, which allowed the doors to be opened in busy streets within the overall width. It too became a Leyland Redline, though the largest versions were given the FJ type tilt cab and became Terriers. Very popular for local delivery work, they lasted until the early 1980s. This is a 1973 550 example for 3.43 tons load/body with the new Leyland 4-98 engine announced in 1972 that developed 69 bhp from 3.77 litres. 2.52 litre diesel and petrol engines were also available.

124. A and B. A special Bear 20 ton gvw chassis appeared in 1969 with 401 engine, Vista-Vue cab, five-speed plus overdrive gearbox and hub reduction axles. Primarily intended for concrete mixers, it was also used for heavy duty tipping. It had a stronger and lighter high-tensile chassis than the Super Comet 20, of which around 1500 had been sold as mixers. A 1965 predecessor is shown with a Barford Rocket mixer. Construction machinery maker Aveling-Barford joined the Leyland group in 1967.

125. Albion ceased to exist as a separate brand in 1972, though its Glasgow factory continued to make components and assemble its own long standing models like the Clydesdale, Chieftain and Reiver. This is a 1975 Clydesdale equipped for snow ploughing and gritting. It had 132 bhp 401 or turbocharged 144 bhp 410 diesels, five- or nine-speed plus overdrive gearboxes and Albion drive axle. The latest re-trimmed version of the old BMC cab was now called the G.

126. Another old BMC model that received a new lease of life as a Leyland was the WF Redline. It covered 3.6 to 11.6 ton gvw models built primarily for export and was produced at Bathgate until replaced by the Landmaster in August 1981. 3000 WFs were sold in its final year. The new model and its immediate predecessor generally used the 6.98 115 bhp diesel or its turbocharged 145 bhp derivative.

The Leyland 'Specials' range

Heaviest of the Leyland Specials, Contractor is used as a road train locomotive by operators such as Wynns, Pickfords and Sunter Bros as well as specialist operators in the mining, logging and oilfield businesses.

Before the Leyland acquisition of Scammell, the Supra-National Oil companies like Contractor. Companies such as Shell and Kuwait Oil Company had as many as ten drilling strings (total vehicle fleets to transport oilfield equipment in its entirety). Such concerns might now only operate one 'string' and the native contractors in the oilfield countries have become the new customers.

Here the need to change from six to four wheel drive arose and the Contractor series was developed as a 6 x 4 configuration with a rear bogie ground load capability of no less than 40.64 tonne. This permits imposed loads through the fifth wheel king pin of 32.5 tonne. The uncomplicated design of this on-highway tractor (with limited off-road capability) has since widened the acceptance of Contractor in general extra-heavy haulage, logging, quarrying and military tank transporting.

The second vehicle down the weight scale, but leader of the 'Specials' in cross-country capability is the Super Constructor, sold as a flatbed oilfield transporter or a 'go-anywhere' off-road tractor. It is a 101.7 tonne (100 ton) gross combination weight machine with suspension and drive train uniquely suited to all-terrain mobility. This is the vehicle that gets through when the other heavy off-roaders find the going is too tough.

The Crusader 6 x 4 is next in gross weight capability of the Leyland Specials. Models are available to cater for 44.3/66 tonne (44/65 ton), on/off highway. The main domestic role for the vehicle is heavy machinery carrier for the civil engineering and similar industries but the vehicle is also of importance in transcontinental TIR transport.

With a greater off-road ability than the Crusader, the Leyland LD55 Bush Tractor can haul gross train weights up to 66 tonne (65 ton) with construction plant transport being one of its major roles. An alternative version, the LD55 Dump Truck, for handling payloads up to 14 tonne (13.8 ton) is fitted with a general purpose body which features low body sides for ease of loading by tractor shovel.

Fifth of the Specials, the Nubian Major, is an all-wheel drive high speed middleweight with 12 tonne (11.8 ton) payload capacity. It is sold to Airport authorities as a Crash Tender and operates at 20.83 tonne (20.5 ton) gross vehicle weight. This vehicle has a highly developed lightweight flexible chassis frame stressed to "ride the bumps" and maintain wheel-to-ground contact at high speeds across country.

127. At various times trucks that were known in Britain under the name of the factory that produced them were sold abroad with the better known Leyland badge. Scammell Contractor ultra-heavyweights were often designated Leylands and this page from a 'Leyland Scammell Special Operation Vehicles' catalogue shows one at the top. At different times in its career the LD55 came with AEC, Thornycroft, Aveling-Barford or Leyland badges. It started life as an AEC Dumptruk chassis and was used in the 1970s as a 25 tonne gvw truck (left) or 66 tonne (gtw) tractive unit (one up from the Thornycroft Nubian crash tender). It used the Leyland (AEC) AV760 212 bhp diesel, whilst the Crusader above it could have many different engines, including the 305 bhp Detroit in the example shown.

128. A and B. Various Austin-Morris vans survived the transition to Leyland, including the 'box on wheels' forward-control EA (shown here in Ilford service) and the J4. The latter was extensively redesigned in 1974 as the Leyland Sherpa. In 1980 a new Freight-Rover division was formed to make and market the Sherpa within the Land-Rover group (itself a Leyland subsidiary). Here we have a high-cube Hawson Garner bodied example. The EA was replaced by versions of the Sherpa, which in 1983 was joined by larger models with twin rear tyres.

129. Ashok Leyland had produced 100 000 heavy vehicles by 1979 and over 12 000 per year thereafter. It employed 6200 men and made vehicles like the Leyland Comet with 125 bhp 400 engine shown here using locally produced components. Local capital was added in 1984 to reduce Leyland's majority shareholding to 40 per cent and to increase output by stages to 40 000 trucks and buses per year. Numerous other Leyland-based vehicles are produced worldwide.

130. The 1964 Sankey-built Leyland cab suitably updated lasted in some cases into the 1980s on models like the Buffalo, Bison and revived Octopus. The range is too familiar to require more than one reference photograph. It shows a Buffalo 2 32 ton artic, available either with the 209 bhp TL11 turbocharged 11.1 litre six-cylinder unit or the naturally aspirated L12 version of the Marathon engine developing 203 bhp that was available from 1976.

Leyland

131. A revised and updated Marathon 2 was sold from 1978. Cummins engines had joined the TL12 in the original model to increase compatibility with fleets that contained Cummins-powered Guys (which were being phased out) and non-Leyland makes. The Marathon 2 also offered Rolls-Royce diesels for similar reasons. This is a fleet working in Belgium in 1978. Marathon six-wheelers were also built with engines of up to 328 bhp.

132. Leyland has numerous affiliated companies in Africa. For example, it makes the Cummins 290 bhp engined Panda in Zimbabwe, employs 650 men in Kenya, and has extensive facilities in Nigeria, where this photo was taken. The last of the traditional bonneted range was built in England in 1979, being replaced by various Scammell models and the Leyland Landtrain of 1980 shown here second from right. The Landtrain usually has Cummins 240 or 290 bhp diesels, ZF or Fuller gearboxes and is for 30 tonnes gvw (up to 65 tonnes gtw).

133. A massive expansion campaign in the late 1970s boosted the Lancashire factories' output to 425 vehicles per week and Bathgate to 17 000 per year. Unfortunately this move coincided with the recession and despite closing most other plants (apart from Scammell and Albion), Leyland output in Britain in 1982 was down to 6000. However, in the depth of the difficulties that this created, Leyland successfully launched its major T45 Roadtrain in 1980. It used the TL12 or Cummins engines, with Rolls-Royce diesels standardised in 1982. This example has an Eagle 265L unit.

134. The G cab had a final update in September 1980 and was then identifiable by the new flush lettering and matt black backing that increased the family likeness to the last of the Ergomatics. This is a 24 ton gvw Perkins V8 engined Super Mastiff with Fuller nine-speed gearbox.

135. The T45's Motor Panels cab could be altered in width and depth to suit long distance/local and day/sleeper requirements. The wide version was used on the Roadtrain and the Constructor eight wheeler that replaced the Octopus and Scammell Routeman as well as the earlier AEC Mammoth Major and Guy Big J. Narrow versions were first provided on the Cruiser 28-34 ton artic range with TL11 engines in 1981, then moved down the weight range to the Constructor six wheeler in late 1981, and came to the Freighters in the following year. This is a Freighter 13.11 (13 tonnes gross, 110 bhp) which replaced one of the previous Boxers.

136. The G cab continued to be provided behind the massive bonnet of the Landtrain, and also behind the more modest 115 bhp 6.98 engine of the Landmaster that replaced the WF in August 1981. Early ones were made at the Guy factory, but following its closure production moved to Bathgate. The Landmaster came in 9 and 12 tonne gvw versions, the latter being shown here.

137. The most significant Leyland in recent times has been the Roadrunner launched in late 1984 and here shown on a road-shock simulator at Leyland's £32 million Technical Centre (photographed somewhat surreptitiously by Nick Baldwin!). Most versions could be driven on a non-HGV licence and had adjustable controls to suit the posture of car or truck drivers. The kerb-spotting window is a distinctive feature, though this was deleted from the ones marketed by DAF under their own name in Europe from 1987. In August 1986 the original Leyland engines were replaced by the new Cummins B-series 115 and 130 bhp diesels developed in conjunction with Leyland, and by then nearly five thousand Roadrunners had been built.

138. The Comet and Super Comet names were revived in 1986 on a range of tough export trucks. The traditional need for bonnets in Third World markets was gradually declining (thanks in part to the success of various Albion-derived forward control models) and Leyland decided that the time was right for a no-frills vehicle bearing a strong family resemblance to the Freighter and Roadrunner. With the closure of the Bathgate factory the Comets entered production in Lancashire. Developed at a cost of nearly £6 million they were available with two or three axles for up to 24 tonnes GVW.

139. Leyland's thoroughly practical approach to the future. The company's ideas for a distribution truck of tomorrow shown for the first time at the NEC 1986. It features six on-board computers, independent suspension, disc brakes, front and rear axle steering, aluminium chassis, infinitely variable transmission and a host of other advanced features. The shape of things to come!

Postscript

Following General Motors' abortive takeover bid for Leyland in 1986 and GM's subsequent closure of most of the Bedford truck operations it looks as though Leyland's future in a declining European truck market is assured. Following the disposal of their Multipart and loss-making Bus and Coach companies Leyland is free to concentrate on its principal business. Even before the departure of Bedford and the merger of Ford and IVECO in Britain, Leylands were consistently the best selling trucks in the country, though with less than a fifth of the total market. The announcement that DAF would be putting their weight behind the Roadrunner and buying thousands looks to be the first of a number of co-operative ventures that should see Leyland through safely to the 21st century. Whether it is still largely owned by the British public at that stage or part of a multi-national group is anyone's guess ....